HOW I BEAT SATAN...
AND THE I.R.S.

HOW I BEAT SATAN...AND THE I.R.S.

Mark Emery

ISBN: 0692443517
ISBN-13: 9780692443514

DEDICATION

This book is dedicated to all of the valiant, tireless researchers who have committed themselves to finding the truth and who have suffered in one way or another as a result. Freedom is not free and this book is a 'thank you' to all of those whose research and sacrifice has made this book possible.

CONTENTS

ACKNOWLEDGMENTS

THE FOLLOWING INDIVIDUALS ARE JUST a few of the daring souls who have influenced me and risked life and limb to 'unravel the code' to bring truth and liberty to those who would seek it: Leroy Schweitzer, Joe Holland, Lindsey Springer, Frank Elena, Dana Dudley, Russ Landers, Hartford VanDyke, Tommy 'TreasuryGate' Buckley, Howard Freeman, Phil & Marlene Marsh, George Gordon, Don Wiedeman, Dr. Eugene Schroder, Jack McLamb and many others.

May God bless us all.

PREFACE

THIS SHORT BOOKLET WILL BRING light and clarity to a murky and very dark subject matter which very few understand. We will be discussing legal concepts in general terms, but don't worry! Not only will it be easily understood and digested, but as your knowledge and understanding increases, so will your excitement when you start to feel the power that your newfound knowledge will bring you. Once you begin to see the power that you actually have, against what you thought was an unbeatable Goliath, this book should be FUN to follow and you will be eager for more!

Disclaimer: I am not a licensed attorney, nor do I have a formal education as offered by the higher educational institutions of today. This is my advantage! It is why I have been so effective in applying what I have learned. I am not programmed to support the status quo. I can think for myself, outside the box and see the entire picture, not just how the 'code' works to support 'the system'.

Even though I have been in many courtrooms running circles around the so called full time 'professionals', I am not engaged in the business of offering legal advice, nor is this book to be construed as a 'How To' book, nor should anybody act on the information contained herein without further study to have a complete command of the subject matter. The information offered in this book is for 'entertainment and 'enlightenment' purposes only' It represents a personal testimony about my own private adventures and what I have learned from that life experience. Everything contained herein I have applied in my life in one way or another with success.

Thus, this is not a textbook based on what 'should work' in theory. With this book I share my story, what I have done and what has worked for me years ago. There is no guarantee that it will work for anyone else. I share this with you freely for the purpose of opening your mind to the possibilities that come with acquired knowledge and its application in life.

The information contained herein is NOT complete. The concepts presented here are GENERAL and INTRODUCTORY in nature and anyone who chooses to 'use' this information for anything other than personal information, education and entertainment, does so at their own risk.

Therefore, as a part of the ONE FREEMAN'S WAR book series, you should consider this volume as a compendium of the several STRATEGIC OPTIONS which have been used and could be available for consideration and further study. As a free people, (if that is in fact, the case) we need to expand our knowledge in the private and collective defense from those who would war against us, the peace loving and free people of the republic of the united States of America.

The 'tactical' operations (details) of the various strategies I have used and which are presented here, can be further explored either at:

www.onefreemanswar.com or www.lighthouseliberty.club

I invite you to continue on this adventure and further develop your knowledge with the resources available in the links above.

To get a better perspective on who I am and where I'm coming from, I would highly recommend the first book in this series:

ONE FREEMAN'S WAR -
IN THE SECOND AMERICAN REVOLUTION

You can find it on amazon.com or onefreemanswar.com That book is a real eye opener.   If you're looking for jaw dropping adventure and revelations of secrets being kept from you by the powers that be, be sure to add it to your bookshelf.

INTRODUCTION

THERE ARE VERY FEW, IF any, institutions in world history which have created as much chaos, pain, destruction, suffering and even death as has the Internal Revenue Service. The IRS is the private collection agency of the Federal Reserve banking system (another private entity), located primarily, but not exclusively, in the U.S.A.

"The way to crush the bourgeoisie
is to grind them between the millstones
of taxation and inflation." - Vladimir Lenin

Chief Justice John Marshall was at his best in the Supreme Court opinion set forth in *McCulloch v. Maryland* in which he used the now famous quote from Daniel Webster:

"The power to tax is the power to destroy"

And in that regard, volumes have already been written about the lives, the businesses, the marriages, the families and the futures of untold victims who have been destroyed.

So before we get into the substance of this book, we need to first explore the 'morality' of this tax issue and discover, or confirm, what exactly is your 'moral obligation' as it relates to 'paying your fair share'. We'll deal with 'legalities' later in the book.

The commonly heard pablum of today goes like this: *"Well, everyone has to pay their fair share to keep the government going and I'm happy to support and do my part."*

Wow! It's hard to know where to even begin addressing the naiveté of such a statement, but let's try to just scratch the surface just a little bit.

#1 Has anyone ever actually defined what 'fair share' even means? No. This is purely subjective. The term is an undefined fiction lodged in the minds of the people who use it. This term would be very clear if the government would actually impose a lawful 'direct tax' which is apportioned among the people as per latest census figures. But this is NOT the tax which is levied on (so called) income, and is never used. So, the term 'fair share' goes undefined and is thus certifiably unachievable.

It has been said that the current national debt amounts to about $60,000 for every man, woman and child in the country. So that would mean that the 'fair share' of a family of 4 is about $240,000, nearly a quarter of a million dollars.

So if paying your fair share is one of your objectives, I guess you could send a check and be done with it! However this does not consider unfunded liabilities which are far greater and literally of amounts so great, they can never be honored and paid. It is simply mathematically impossible. So how do you pay your fair share of that which is impossible even if it were defined?

#2 What you pay to the I.R.S. does NOT go to the federal government. The 'Internal Revenue' is a private trust operated secretly from it's domicile of Puerto Rico, a federal corporate enclave. This fact is confirmed in writing in the Code of Federal Regulations (C.F.R.s) and also in Title 31 of the U.S. Code section 1321 where research to which IRS officials have acquiesced suggests that the Secretary exercised his authority as trustee of Puerto Rico Trust #62 (Internal Revenue).

As mentioned previously, the I.R.S. is a private collection agency for the private 'family owned' business known as the Federal Reserve. I trust you already understand that. If not, plenty of well documented books are available to explain in further detail. So the I.R.S. basically serves three purposes;

A) as a collection agency for a family business, to take the wealth of the people as compensation for the ridiculous debt the federal government incurs on the back of the taxpayers. This debt is false and there is no need for it to occur if money was 'spent' into circulation and not 'lent'. But that opens up an entirely different can of worms we can't get into here.

B) it operates to siphon off a large percentage of the cash from the economy for the simple purpose of hiding what would be a tell tale sign of the false money system they operate. That 'tell tale sign' would be 'hyperinflation'. The way that money is created in this false money system (false weights and measures by biblical standards), hyperinflation would be the inevitable and natural consequence and would make the lifespan of the system very short lived.

So then, by skimming money out of the economy, it becomes a mechanism to keep the money in circulation somewhat restricted, thus holding off the hyperinflation (for a time) which would be otherwise inevitable sooner rather than later.

C) And lastly, of course, the system is one of 'control'. It is a direct invasion of privacy and is an affront to the concept of private property. As we have seen in recent news headlines, it is used as a very effective weapon against select political enemies.

Now, let's get personal. Let me show you how this private group of profiteers is stealing the future from your family.

Let's say that over the course of your working career, your average annual net taxable income (after deductions) is $45,000. In a 45 year career, a simple tax rate of 20% would amount to $9,000 a year or $405,000 over 45 years.

Now, let's take into consideration the time value of money and say that had you kept that money yourself and only earned a humble 8% annually (a common figure in annuities). Pro-rated with interest paid monthly, the actual time adjusted, compounded value of what you have given up is approximately $4.2 million!

If you have a two income household you can double that figure!

Now, did your parents have over $4 million to share with you when they retired? Of course not, because they were busy paying 'their fair share'. A family could use this lost patrimony to: be debt free, to buy a new home, debt free, to create and build a business, debt free, to be financially independent (and debt free!), to help the less fortunate in the community and reduce government dependency and debt (control).

With this kind of savings rate by the entire population, the community bank would be flush with deposits to lend back into the community on easy terms to create a vibrant local economy and opportunities for all! I'm envisioning a land of milk and honey!

Now, in contrast, look at the national debt that each baby born today is inheriting and enslaved to. Look at your local economy and employment rate. Look at the declining level of prosperity and opportunity for the 'average citizen' in your area. Look at what independent businesses are facing with over reaching regulations and interference in the local marketplace. Look at what Obamacare alone is doing to both businesses and individuals.

In view of this, honestly, what does the future look like for your children from your perspective?

Now let me ask you an important question. What is your priority? To take care of your family? Or do you prefer to take care of someone else or other nefarious, morally objectionable projects at the expense of your family?

That 'someone else' would be the likes of; millions of new illegal aliens, 'moderate Islamic radicals' which are being funded, foreign aid to anti-American countries because it's good business, Planned Parenthood dismemberment chambers, the military industrial complex, political pet 'green' projects like 'Solyndra' which get paid hundreds of millions in taxpayer funds largely for the benefit of the executives only to go bankrupt, and the like.

Who is paying the price for this idea of 'paying your fair share' to a private group of mafiosos? Where is the moral value in that? Something to think about.

Thankfully, my understanding of the law enabled me to make my choices with full legal support. I discovered 'who I was' and 'to whom I belonged' and that resolves the legal issues right there.

**"Thou shalt make no covenants with them
(alien governments), nor their gods."
- Exodus 23:32**

Otherwise, my personal moral objections would have forced me to violate the law, and I would have, without hesitation. But it wasn't necessary.

I fight to support, promote and encourage all that is good, honest and productive And what is good comes from God the father. Therefore, it only follows in logic that I stand against anything to the contrary!

We know that God created man in his own image and all that God created was good. Now, to the contrary, we know that Satan is warring against God, and only one entity in existence despises God and his fruit (man) to the point of wanting to destroy it all. That entity is Satan. Therefore, since the I.R.S. is based purely on fraud and deception with the power to destroy and not do good, we can logically deduce without any doubt that Satan and the I.R.S. are inextricably linked. Thus, the title of the book Anyone who would argue the point is simply not well informed.

Let's get down to practical matters starting with the first chapter...

CHAPTER 1
CONCLUSION

YOU ARE LIKELY THINKING THAT it's a bit odd that a book starts with the Conclusion. Most books start laying foundation, creating interest, developing the characters, generating a logical sequence to follow upon which they build the story to the dramatic conclusion at the end!

Not here. As you can tell from the introduction, I do things a little bit differently.

I'm going to tell you right up front what it takes to beat Satan himself and his minions in the I.R.S. Once you have the solution up front, you can decide if that suits you or not and whether or not it would be worth reading the rest of the book. At least, when you see the simple solution to this problem, you will know if you are wasting your time with the rest of the book or not. I'm just trying to help you out here.

So when I tell you how simple it is to beat the I.R.S., if you buy into it, you can read further and we'll expand on a few key 'demon killer' concepts all of which I've used myself in one way or another to keep the demons away.

If you don't see yourself getting any benefit, or not being able to do what is necessary, then you can toss the whole thing and save yourself some time. I kept the price low for just such a purpose.

Here it is. Are you ready?

There are only two ways the I.R.S. can nail you.

#1   Civil Action.   They like to take your stuff!
#2   Criminal Action.   They like to throw you in jail.

Block these two roads that they travel on and you are home free, forever! And let me tell you from experience, it's not that difficult as you will see.

Regarding #1 Civil Action: If you position yourself so that you have nothing they can grab, you are free from any effects from a civil case. You have to structure your life so that you don't own any property in your name or have any income to speak of which can be attached. It's easier than you might think for some people who are more independent. For others, perhaps not so much but we have 'other' ways, so sit tight.

Now don't get too worried about owning nothing and having no income. I know you are envisioning yourself with matted hair, living in a box under the bridge! But that's not what I'm talking about. Whew! eh?

It's really a simple matter of 'Being a pauper on paper yet living like a King!' as W.G. Hill, author of 'The PT' used to say.

Personally, I own nothing of value and have no personal income. I don't care that I don't own anything. I live in a mansion on a mountaintop, drive new cars and travel frequently to exotic locations, all paid for by friends, sponsors and collaborators.

Do I care if my name is on the title of this house or the cars I use? I live here anyway. I enjoy it just the same. In fact, I enjoy it more knowing that if someone wants to pick a fight with me, they won't get anything because I don't own anything. That is a much more relaxing way to live!

Hillary would say, "What difference does it make?" Yet since I've positioned myself this way, I live like a King of Kings and have far surpassed my wildest dreams of how beautiful my life is, living in God's paradise. More on this later.

Yes, I know the I.R.S. has spies who follow you around to compare your lifestyle to your reported income, but have some patience here. Who cares? We haven't even begun yet. I was a Boy Scout and you know what that means.... I come prepared!

Regarding #2 Criminal Action: To be convicted of a crime the burden is on the prosecution to show that you 'knowingly, willingly and intentionally' did in fact violate the law with the intention of inuring some benefit for yourself. The key to proving a crime here is 'intent'.

This is so easy to defeat it's child's play. You do it in advance, before any courtroom scenario develops. You do it by setting the record with documentation (information request letters, affidavits, notices, etc.) showing your willingness and strong desire to be compliant with the law, if only they could answer a couple of questions to clarify things for you!

When you ask for help, stating your good intentions, you are acting in good faith. When they don't help you, <u>they</u> are not acting in good faith.

When they don't answer your questions, your only option is to establish that your presumptions must be correct and then, this is the prima facie case. I'll be showing you several examples.

The law is so fraught with fraud, exceptions, errors, inconsistencies and gaps, the I.R.S. has no possible way to respond to your questions for clarity because if they did, they would admit fraud and have to acquiesce to your 'exempt' status. Thus, they will acquiesce every time to your prima facie case, and your record is set, permanently!

You tried in good faith! You tried again! And you're still trying to comply with the law, but the I.R.S. just refuses to cooperate so we have no choice but to presume that your assertions are correct unless or until rebutted by affidavit or material evidence. And they can't! You know it and they know it.

It's really fun because you know the result before you even send the letter! The process is just a formality to create evidence in your favor. Once they know that you are on to their fraud, they usually stop harassing you and they go look for some other lost sheep who have strayed from the corral and are easy prey.

They can't throw you in jail for acting in good faith and for trying to comply with the law! The law simply cannot require the impossible!

And when you set the record with your documentation which is done properly with care, not only will you never see the inside of a jail cell, but you will never see the inside of a courtroom because they don't dare bring you and your documentation into a court of public record to expose the fraud to the entire world!

Now, if you can't change your work and income structure, don't fret. We'll get into other things you can do without changing anything in your current job and income profile. There are options!

There you have it. That's how to beat Satan himself and his I.R.S. minions!

Can you handle it? If not, thanks for buying the book and getting this far. You can toss the book now. and save some time

If you want more, then let's start getting into some details and continue to the next chapter....

CHAPTER 2

THE LAW MERCHANT

THIS IS THE KEY, THE missing link and the secret which has allowed government to deny you of your inherent birthrights and to control your life. What is The Law Merchant or Lex Mercantoria?

The Law Merchant is defined as:

"The system of rules and customs and usages generally recognized and adopted by traders as the law for the regulation of their commercial transactions and the resolution of their controversies. The law merchant is codified in the Uniform Commercial Code (UCC), a body of law, which has been adopted by the states, that governs mercantile transactions."

Ever since House Joint Resolution 192 was passed by congress in 1933 the gold standard was suspended and they abrogated the gold clause (real money) in the constitution. Now, when they took the next step in 1968 and removed the silver redemption feature from the money in circulation, the people could no longer 'pay debts' at law, but instead were actors in commerce who had the 'privilege' or 'franchise' of limited liability and could only then 'discharge the liability' with Federal Reserve Notes (promises to pay which never get paid).

Why is this important and how does it affect us? Because by virtue of this 'franchise privilege', which is forced upon everyone through our use of the federal reserve notes and other actions, this puts us in law as a 'merchant' who is thus governed by the Law Merchant in everything we do.

Congress can regulate commerce. It can't regulate 'real people' living among the several states. Therefore, we have been suckered into a situation where we are no longer dealt with as 'real' people, but we have become a 'legal person' just like a corporation and everything we do is considered 'commerce'. Thus everything we do is subject to the U.S. Inc. corporate bylaws (legislative code), which normally would only apply to officials and corporations in Washington, D.C. and the territories (by law).

The net result for you is that The Law Merchant (what I call the 'public' side of the law) now replaces the common law where substance and God given rights are recognized (what I call the 'private' side of the law). In other words, you no longer are recognized as having God given rights and are not subject to the common law, where things make sense, rely upon substance and where there is no crime without a damaged party.

Under the Law Merchant, courts can make summary judgement upon you without jury trial. They can impose regulations, fees, fines, mandates and all sorts of obligations through compelled performance statutes, forcing you to do things, to pay for things, to submit to things that you have absolutely no interest in.

Do you see how this works? As an 'individual' John Smith, under the Fifth Amendment to the constitution for the united States of America, cannot be compelled to witness against himself (i.e. file a disclosure form like the 1040). This is the common law here the federal government has no jurisdiction.

However, as a legal fiction or juristic 'person' JOHN SMITH operating under the Law Merchant, is subject to the corporate mandates and 'compelled performance statutes' whether he likes it or not. Go look at all your correspondence from 'official' government entities and corporations and notice how your name is spelled.

This is why, in the organic republic form of government, Man is the creator and master of the government. And this is also why, now under the Law Merchant, the 'created' is now lord over its 'creator' and government lords itself over man.

Things are twisted and upside down due to this situation, just as it was foretold it would be in the last days.

There are some fascinating videos on the Birth Certificate, and it explains how 'Your Name' became a 'legal person' represented by YOUR NAME and related subject matter. You can find this on the 'Resources' page of www.onefreemanswar.com. You are encouraged to have a look.

The Lighthouse Law Club provides much more information on this and other important subject matter should you choose to continue your study further. See www.lighthouseliberty.club

In this short space we haven't even been able to give a good introduction on this important subject matter. However, if your interest is piqued, read the short article <u>Two Sides of the Law</u> on www.onefreemanswar.com It makes things very clear in practical terms.

By the way, The Law Merchant is used worldwide in nearly all countries and is not particular to the USA. So wherever you are from, or living, it applies to you too so pay attention!

CHAPTER 3

SELF DISCOVERY - WHO AM I?

ON MY OWN ROAD TO personal self discovery, my spirituality has been awakened, discovered and developed enough that I walk in faith and confidence to the point where I 'expect' miracles when I need them. They always happen when needed the most and I have more testimonies to the greatness of God than I can write here. Suffice it to say that because I know who I am, and who I belong to I have no fear of what this world wants to do to me. I've been there and done that!

Who would publish a book, telling the world how he beat the I.R.S.? Countless others have tried and now sit in jail at this moment. I could make a list of several whom I know personally. Am I a fool? Possibly.

Or do I walk with strength in truth, in law and with the power of the Holy Spirit which is in me knowing that my adversaries who plot against me cannot hold a candle to HE who is in me? Whichever is true, make no mistake, I stand on my beliefs and will die with them. Everything else in between is just 'motion'. I invite others to stand with me.

I can only encourage you to work on developing this same inner strength because we are truly fighting against the principalities of darkness in this world, in all facets of life. Dealing with satan's minions in government are only some of the most obvious. And that's not to say that all people working in government are evil, because they are not. I am thankful for all of the good people trying to do a good job and there

8

are many. We need you! And we need you to make a difference by your example!

But the system, as it is being applied and directed today surely is satan's tool and you won't be successful defending yourself against it without inner strength, conviction and an ability to be 'bold'. Your peers and probably your family will not understand and you will be castigated and marginalised in many cases.

If anyone is to be taken captive, to captivity he goes:
if anyone is doomed to death by sword, with the sword he must be
slain. Here is a call for the endurance and faith of the saints.
- Revelations 13:10

When the issue of taxation comes up, I have heard far too many times, Christians making blind reference to Romans 13 which includes: "Render unto Caesar what is Caesar's" and they take a 'one size fits all' approach with a simplistic, superficial interpretation which they apply in broad strokes to everything, without the benefit of any analysis, context or true understanding what is really being said.

Now God gave me a mind and I intend on being a good steward so I will use it! Combined with guidance of the Holy Spirit I have the following revelations to share with you.

Romans 13 takes great pains in differentiating 'good' from 'evil'. See for yourself. Why would this be if it weren't important in understanding the context of the message? When we discuss 'paying tribute to higher authorities because they are 'ordained of God', the premise is that 'they are ordained to do good under God's authority'. One could never argue against that.

Now, what do we do when it becomes clear that the ruling authorities are the minions of satan himself and are actively destroying all that is good that comes from God? As a good Christian are you going to ignore the wilful destruction of the Christian community? It's happening right now! If you don't believe it, you need to pull your head out of the sand and look around a little bit. The signs are everywhere and I'm not going to take time pointing out the obvious here.

Should the Christians in Syria, Iran and Egypt and elsewhere in the Mid-East pay tribute to support the ruling ISIS as their families are being tortured and beheaded on Sunday afternoons as a public spectacle and their heads are put on spikes surrounding the public park? Is ISIS ordained of God to do good to the brothers and sisters? Let's pay tribute! Come on people! Give unto Caesar!

We can obviously see how ridiculous it is to give blind, universal acquiescence to the concept of 'Give unto Caesar' in all cases without the context and premises given to us very clearly in Romans 13.

Modern society is systematically dismembering Christian values and heritage at every opportunity. Did you know that U.S. military and federal agency training manuals openly list 'Evangelical Christians' and 'Patriots' who believe in the constitution and the bible' as **'enemies of the state'** on a par with terrorists? Do your research. It's there.

Will Christians continue to do nothing and lie passively in their prone position and willingly submit to pure evil because they don't have the discernment or the interest or the courage to take the time and truly understand Romans 13? This, of course would be a 'cop out' and an abdication of your responsibility to 'do the right thing'. This passivist, cop out attitude is far too popular by the lukewarm, milk toast Christian community these days!

"Do you not know that if you yield yourselves to anyone
as obedient slaves, you are slaves of the one whom you obey,
either of sin, which leads to death,
or of obedience which leads to righteousness."
- Romans 6:16

In law, 'failure to object' is fatal and 'silence is consent'! Where do you think this legal concept comes from? This is biblical as well. If you fail to stop a rape when you had the chance, you are as guilty of the rape as the perpetrator!

Did Jesus come in peace? No. He came with a sword to divide and separate. Are you of his sheep, or of the goats? Will you grab your sword and help Jesus separate? In this process, we will discover 'who is who' and you might even discover 'who are you', if you haven't already.

Having said that, I have no desire to imply that one should not 'pay tribute' where tribute is due. This is where it is critically important for us to know 'who we are' and 'when' and 'to whom' the obligation of 'tribute' is required so that all 'tribute due' is honored and paid as required and that all lawful obligations are honored and met.

Personally, I pay every single cent of tribute that the law requires of me and not a penny less. In fact, just to avoid any doubt, I have been known to pay even more than required. True story. But because I understand who I am and to whom, and how the law applies, thankfully, my legal requirement is -0- as it relates to Subtitle A, 1040 income taxes. More on that later.

Look at Matthew 17:25:

> *Jesus spoke "What do you think Simon?*
> *From whom do the kings of the earth take toll or tribute?*
> *From their sons or from others?*
> Simon said, "From others." Jesus said to him, "Then the sons are free."

From this we can easily deduce that if truly, the powers that be are ordained of God to do his will, and you are in fact and in law, a son or daughter of God, then you should be free! Those words come from Jesus, not me folks!

So then it only follows that if you are in fact, and in law 'not free', then what does this mean? Either you, or your government are a 'foreigner' to God and we have a conflict don't we? Do you see how dangerous it is to be 'lost' and not aware of your true character or to whom you really belong?

We can further study this issue in:

Exodus 30:12-15 and Numbers 3:40-51 which discusses lawful taxa-tion in the poll tax (head tax) being levied and it should be a small amount. The poll tax is based on census (direct apportionment as in the U.S.A. constitution) and all men are subject to pay the same small amount regardless of income. This is a correct tax according to the bible (and the constitution for the U.S. of A.)

Deut. 16:17, 1 Corinthians 16:1-2 discusses that every man shall give as he is able according to the blessings God has given him (ad valorem tax).

1 Kings 12:13-19 discusses abusive and heavy taxation leads to rebel-lion by the people.

Nehemiah 5: 1-5 discusses the Kings taxes have caused an impov-erished nation, slavery and destruction of the families, brothers and sisters.

Nehemiah 9: 32-37 discusses how oppressive taxation is often due to the sins of the nation,

Which brings us to Revelation 18:4

'Come out of her my people so that you will not share in her sins,
so that you will not receive any of her plagues,"

Personally, I have 'come out of her' spiritually, legally and physically in very practical terms. I have removed myself from the legalistic phari-sees and their schemes and have been blessed in ways that defy descrip-tion, as a result.

And lastly, we refer to 1 Corinthians 7:22,23 which states:

"...if you can get your freedom get it.
The person who was a slave when God called him is now the Lord's freeman.
In the same way, the person who was a freeman when God called him is now Christ's slave. Christ paid a price for you; don't be slaves of men."

Only you can determine 'who you are' and how you are governed.

Only you can decide for yourself what your moral, and legal obligations are. That's not for me to say. There are no 'simple tricks' to avoid paying taxes that are legally due. There are no 'magic documents' that release you from your legal obligations. You need to pay what is legally due. I do.

The whole point of this book is, that with some diligence on your part, you can better understand what might be due or not due, according to the law. And you may be able to lawfully change your 'modus operandi' so that those 'legal obligations' may not apply to you in the future, if they ever did in the first place!

Without a fundamental and spiritually sound understanding of who you are, who you belong to and how you relate to this world, playing 'tricks' on the 'powers that be' will only get you in trouble. Everything starts with spiritual discernment and the confidence that only faith in God can provide. Without that, you may not have the strength or guidance to prevail in a contentious situation when fighting against the principalities of darkness.

CHAPTER 4

STAYING OUT OF COURT

BEING HAULED INTO COURT CAN strike fear into the hearts of the most stout of us. First, few people have the money to hire the top attorneys. And once you understand that you are likely to never win with an attorney and you have to go it alone to have a proper defense, going into foreign territory with little training or experience becomes a daunting task for most.

Having said that, there are those among us (pro se litigants) who are not licensed attorneys but are well read and studied enough that an invitation to court is as good as being invited to a football game!

We love the competition, especially when we win after watching the opponent turn red in the face, blow steam out their ears and generally become dumbfounded by the fact that a 'bozo' comes in off the street and makes the professionals look like undisciplined school kids! Fun! Fun! Fun! This was what I did for recreation for several years.

We don't have the space for that here, but my book ONE FREEMAN'S WAR IN THE SECOND AMERICAN REVOLUTION goes into that topic at great length with a variety of entertaining stories.

But those kinds of people are few and far between and the odds are, that going to court could possibly give you a heart attack, so let's stay on point.

Staying out of court is a relatively easy thing to accomplish and we can choose any one of several methods to achieve success if we just understand two fundamental issues.

First, we have to understand that even for the government, which has unlimited resources, they do have limits on personnel and other resources like courtroom dockets etc. so they have to choose their cases wisely to get the best return on the investment and keep the machine well oiled and running smoothly. They seek a) high conviction rates, and b) highest average amount of 'plunder' 'er I mean 'collections' per customer.

Remember, you're dealing with the mafia here, so 'government' is not there to help you! Government is a 'business' to make money. The sooner you understand that, the quicker you will be getting to the root of any given matter which comes up.

Secondly, most government prosecutors are not interested in 'justice'. They are interested in advancing their careers. To do that, they need 'bonus points' on the 'monthly sales leader board' for *most convictions* regardless of the facts of the cases. They don't care if you become the grist of the mill so long as you serve 'their' purposes which are; money, glory and career.

I have personally witnessed government prosecutors and witnesses (i.e. police, agents et al) talking in the antechambers of the courtroom about how they were going to 'engineer' the testimony to get the conviction, regardless of the acknowledged innocence of the defendant. And then they discussed how they were going to divide the 'spoils' amongst themselves. I heard it with my own ears! Don't kid yourself!

Whenever you see a courtroom, just imagine in your mind's eye, how the livestock are herded into the slaughterhouse one by one and then 'processed'! Enough said.

Why are these two points important?

As we discussed previously, if you can make yourself an 'unattractive customer' by having little if anything which they can take, then you are not worth the investment that a court case requires and you become disqualified from consideration! That would apply to civil cases.

Where criminal charges may be involved, think about that 'Monthly Sales Leader Board' that your prosecutor has in his bosses office! A difficult case can drag on for months and eat up valuable time. Remember, 'Time is money' and to the mafiosos, money is their god. If they lose.... look out!

This time lost on a difficult case could otherwise be invested in three or four 'slam dunk' cases foisted upon the ignorant, which all add to the all important monthly sales totals!

So then, when you have properly set your paperwork in advance, you will have raised issues which they will NEVER bring into a court of public record because it would expose their scam. If the court record reflects fraud and misapplication of the law, causing havoc and chaos amongst the people of the land and word got out..... they'd be out of business, period! It's likely they'd be hung from the nearest tree!

This is the power that you have. It is at your doorstep. Use it!

CHAPTER 5

NOTICE OF OFFER
OF PERFORMANCE

THIS DOCUMENT AND PROCESS IS by far one of my favorite ones to use. (the others mentioned in this book are my other favorites!). The Notice of Offer of Performance (NOPE) is eloquent, elegant, it is humble, simple and straightforward. It effectively illustrates my eternal good faith and all the while it packs the punch of a Cesium trigger in a NATO warhead and nobody has ever wanted to touch it or even come close. Can you imagine that?

Here's how it works:

The IRS sends me a notice that I owe them money.

I send a reply in response, indicating that I am more than happy to offer to 'extinguish this obligation' and I tender my 'Offer' to do just that.

It is well established in American Jurisprudence that an obligation is extinguished by an Offer of Performance.

> "A tender is an offer with the intent to extinguish the obligation
> when properly made, it has the effect of putting
> the other party in default if he refuses to accept that,"
> - Heisenberg v. Hirschhorn 275 P 997. 79 Cal 532

My 'Offer' is conditional however. Attached to my reply letter, is an 'Affidavit'. This affidavit, attested to under penalties of 'bearing false witness' (not perjury) of course, establishes my nature as a living breathing 'individual' real person upon the land among the several states and not a corporate, juristic 'PERSON' subject to regulation of The Law Merchant in the jurisdiction in which they operate (Washington, D.C. and the territories).

In American and English jurisprudence, the burden of proof is always on the one making the claim. So if the IRS makes a claim against me, I am within my rights to ask them to substantiate that claim and that's exactly what I do.

I respectfully require them to produce documentation, or documentary evidence or documentary facts relating to 5 key issues, pertaining to me, which I know they simply cannot produce because they don't exist.

In good faith, I request immediate reply but set a date set certain of 30 days for them to get it organized and get back to me. Their objections to my Offer of Performance, if any, must be immediately stated or they must 'forever hold their peace' and they are estopped from ever objecting at some date in the future for any reason.

When the 30 day response time comes and goes without a whimper, as it always does, being the good guy I am I send them a reminder.

My reminder is a 'Notice of Default' and to show my good faith, I extend the deadline and give them another 10 days to reply, just in case they were very busy and forgot about it!

That 10 day period goes by without a whimper and to set the record once and for all time, I send a NOTICE OF DEFAULT and DEFAULT ABSOLUTE, which establishes the fact in the permanent record that my affidavit stands as unrebutted 'Fact', is the Prima Facie case, and I have obliterated their claim against me as it no longer legally exists. They have nothing to stand on and would lose immediately if ever brought into court due to simple operation of basic commercial law.

Should the IRS ever come back and 'refuse' my offer for any reason, I am very happy about that too. Why? The U.C.C. is very clear that 'an

offer to pay any obligation in full which is refused, is a debt paid, at law".
So should they 'refuse' my offer, I send them a thank you letter with a
reminder of the appropriate U.C.C. section and the obligation is extinguished at that time.

End of story.

Oh, and by the way, just so there was no confusion I sent copies of all
correspondence, certified return receipt requested (document identi-
fier number) to my local/regional District case manager, as well as the
Department of the Treasury, I.R.S. in Washington D.C. and the Dept. of
Justice, so they could keep tabs on the operation and no records would
ever be lost!

CHAPTER 6

FILING STATEMENT

PEOPLE GO TO JAIL FOR 'Wilful Failure to File', right?

Some time ago I was made aware that to sign a 1040 form I have to do so under penalty of perjury and that when I sign, I swear that I fully understand everything in, over, under and around the IRC which is roughly 10,000 pages of statutes plus the 30,000+ pages of regulations pertaining to the Internal Revenue Code. When I submit the 1040 I swear upon oath that my 'filing' is correct, complete and accurate as it relates to all of the above. Sign Here!

Ha! Yeah right! The fact of the matter is, that anyone and everyone, including your tax preparer, DOES IN FACT COMMIT PERJURY every time they sign a 1040 form. Nobody can say that they understand the mangrove quagmire of the IRC.

In 1913, in a debate on the Senate floor regarding the first income tax act under the 16th Amendment, Senator Elihu Root commented about the complexity of that first law (back when it was only 80 pages):

"I guess you will have to go to jail if that is the result of not understanding the Income Tax law. I shall meet you there. We shall have
a merry, merry time, for all of our friends will be there. It will be an
intellectual center, for nobody understands the Income Tax Law except
persons who have not sufficient intelligence to understand the questions that arise under it."

I saw a study recently that a taxpayer took his taxes to 20 different tax preparation experts. These experts are full time professionals who know their stuff! Each expert came up with a different result.

Therefore, it goes without saying (but I'll say it anyway) that, in my mind, it is morally and legally WRONG to commit perjury by signing the 1040. But people do it because 'that's what we're supposed to do', right? Oops!

Making false sworn statements is not only a crime, but for us Christians it is also a sin. But people do it anyway. Not me.

It just so happens, that by luck, or by divine providence, or by just plain stubbornness I found an alternative solution to this dilemma which is so beautiful I want to frame my documents and hang them on the wall to admire every day! I get a warm feeling inside just thinking about it!

I'm talking about the 'Filing Statement'. Since I cannot make false declarations by signing a 1040 form for reasons stated, in order to avoid 'Wilful Failure to File' charges I need to 'file' something right? Not really, but just play along.

My 'Filing Statement' is submitted in lieu of the 1040. It is a statement in Affidavit form and is sworn, or 'attested to' under penalties of 'bearing false witness' which is a christian concept as opposed to the 'legislative code' as in 'perjury'.

Title 26 USC section 6012 states that:

> "... every person liable for any income (internal revenue) tax must file a return or 'statement' as provided by law."

So without arguing that I am not <u>one of 'those' persons</u>, I want to just keep it simple. So let's just stay away from that argument and presume that I am 'subject' and that I have every intention of accepting all the false assumptions without argument.

My 'filing statement' includes a memorandum of law relating to the Internal Revenue Code (IRC) and establishes the fact that it is in full compliance with 'the code'. This establishes my good faith having taken the time to understand my legal obligations and intentions to be compliant and their law is on the face of the document.

It then contains a memorandum of law and a long list of case law court decisions which demonstrate a clear dissent of opinion between the brightest legal minds of the country (various federal courts) relating to the controlling statute governing the legal requirements for filing.

This extreme vicissitude of opinion between the various federal courts raises 'clear doubt' (hows that for an oxymoron?) on many substantive issues, which are then raised in my filing statement. Here is one short excerpt from my 5 page detailed filing statement:

"If the Federal District Courts, Tax Court, Court of Claims and the Supreme Court cannot definitively decide the fundamental question as to which section of the Internal Revenue Code requires the filing of an income tax return, whether the tax imposed is an excise or a direct tax, it is obvious that the average American, not educated in the law, will have great difficulty in understanding the tax imposed and this basic question on filing requirements, and the specie of the tax, among many other questions. Since the courts are so deeply split over this issue, how can anyone understand the law in an atmosphere of judicial incertitude? Due process requires that the law be such that the duty imposed is unambiguous and those subject to it are able to understand the law. This is not the case with Title 26 USC or 26 CFR implementing regulations."

My filing statement continues along this thread to finally make the point that in view of the published uncertainty of record, and in the absence of any definitive corrections to the contrary, I am doing my best to comply, as best as I can understand, etc. Therefore, nobody can say that what I am doing is 'Not' correct!

This establishes three things;

A) ...my good faith attempt to comply which eliminates any potential criminal charges for wilful failure to file because of my good faith 'intent'.

B) ...it also puts the IRS on the defensive on many issues raised, with full legal support. And by virtue of being included in my document, which could later be used as evidence in a courtroom, should they ever be nice enough to invite me, it would open up a Pandora's box of issues which the IRS would never allow a jury to even 'hear' let alone determine.

C) ...It drives a silver cross deep into the heart of the beast by asking the simple question: "what law exactly can you point to which requires me to file and where are the implementing regulations?" You will never get an answer to that one, because 'THERE IS NO LAW"! Ask your legal mentor, why there is no such law. The answer is simple and astounding.

And just to show my good faith once again, in the face of complete and overwhelming uncertainty over whether I am liable, and if so, how much I should pay, and on and on, I include a money order payable to the U.S. Treasury for $50 as a good faith gesture to pay 'my fair share'!

There! I filed! I paid my taxes! I exempted myself from being drawn into court and because I have never received any information to the contrary from the IRS about my averments, including the fact that I am not subject to subtitle A (income) taxes, they stand as fact and I am free!

What's for lunch?

"For we did not follow cleverly devised myths when
we made known to you the power and coming
of our Lord Jesus Christ."
II Peter 1:16

"But these, like irrational animals, creatures of instinct,
born to be caught and killed, reviling in the matters
of which they are ignorant, will be destroyed in the same destruction
with them, suffering wrong for their wrongdoing."
-II Peter 2:12

CHAPTER 7

CREATING A PARALLEL EXISTENCE

ONE APPROACH WHICH IS QUITE attractive to people who are pretty well entrenched in their style of life and business and who find it difficult to change their modus operandi, is to create a 'Parallel Existence'.

The concept is simple and despite all my success in the other areas we are discussing, I like to use this one myself for privacy and security purposes as well. Much like the government has created a parallel 'person' by creating the corporate fiction which is 'YOUR NAME', to act in place of 'Your Name', you can do something similar in effect.

For many people there is merit to the strategy of maintaining everything 'status quo' and simply keeping a minimal low profile as it relates to your financial and legal status.

At the same time, through the use of business structures and/or entities which are by law, 'other persons', perhaps even in 'other jurisdictions' and through the use of trusted, licensed nominees as legal representatives, I have had success in using these 'other persons' to suit my goals and ambitions without taking on the personal liability that comes with those activities.

Legitimate business relationships can be set up with these other persons and through continued support and contributions to our common interests, net asset value can grow, businesses can be built, investment portfolios can grow in a secure, low tax environment and all around productivity, or just simple 'safekeeping' can be had in places which are much more friendly to it's people, than what your 'place' might be to 'you'.

There is no 'hiding' involved. There is no 'evasion' involved. It is simply open, up front and honest business relationships that are allowed to develop on 'the other side of the fence' from where you are, where a whole different set of rules apply (for the better).

This does require a little time, expense and travel to set up, but for those who have something worthwhile to protect or develop, it is well worth the nominal investment and can be a lot of fun too!

CHAPTER 8

THE BIGGEST TAX HAVEN
IN THE WORLD

THE WORLD HAS CHANGED DRAMATICALLY in the last 15 years. Financial services and offshore business management used to be a huge, thriving and critical industry for many small nations with little else to offer the world in order to bolster their GDP and financial accounts.

Unfortunately, the western nations of the O.E.C.D. (Organization for Economic Cooperation and Development) led by the U.S.A. began to realize that their oppressive tax and control structures were simply not competitive and they were losing too much business to these more competitive nations.

Rather than reform their systems to keep up with the competition, which is what you do in a 'free market', they went out to 'crush' the competition mafia style. They declared an all out false 'war' on financial freedom and privacy in the name of fighting 'terrorism' and 'money laundering' which provides a convenient (false) backdrop for the effort which is still underway.

This effort is intended to force these other competitive financial regimes to capitulate to 'the new rules' which helps keep the sheep in the corral and offers little more than; increased bureaucracy, more overhead and brow beating, less production, less privacy, less security and more scarce financial services.

Through the recently enacted FATCA (Foreign Account Tax Compliance Act) foreign banks around the world who have U.S.

correspondent bank relationships (nearly all banks worldwide), are now required to search their records for any and all U.S. clients and report all of this information to the I.R.S. or face mortal financial penalties imposed through their U.S. correspondents. The U.S. has no jurisdiction to dictate to other nations, but they do have jurisdiction over the correspondent banks in New York and elsewhere, who deal with the foreign banks.

In other words, through economic coercion, the banksters of the west have brow beaten the entire global financial industry to be unpaid agents and spies for the money powers based in the U.S.A.

Many foreign banks and financial institutions have almost immediately found the perfect solution to this. Rather than deal with the headaches and expense, much of the financial world now simply refuses to deal with anybody who carries a U.S. passport! Problem solved! Financial services around the world are now 'out of reach' for Americans thanks to this effort. American passport? Oops sorry, 'No Soup for You'! Once again, Americans are screwed due to the greed and short sighted, 'brow beating' policies from the bully of the financial world (for the time being).

So much for free and open markets! But then, is this perhaps the end game after all? Keeping the U.S. 'merchants' in the corral might have its benefits for those bankers and governments who are otherwise going bankrupt due to their own policies and shortsightedness.

The hypocrisy is beyond the pale. While claiming to clamp down on tax evasion, unreported assets and income from errant and unrepentant slaves who have left the fold, the West holds itself to a much lower standard than that which it imposes on the rest of the world.

As it relates to attracting foreign capital the draconian standards that the U.S.A. and it's western allies are coercing worldwide, simply do not apply to their own financial regimes.

It is well known that the biggest tax havens in the world are found in the capitals of New York and 'the City' of London.

For example: The United States does not tax non-resident aliens for most interest income or dividend income derived from the United

States. There is zero capital gains on profits from investments for non-resident aliens. There is zero tax on income earned outside the USA. Only active United States derived income is taxed. Also, various tax treaties give a United States company certain tax advantages when doing business outside the USA. Do you have those benefits?

And those reporting requirements the USA is demanding from all banks around the world? The U.S. can't be bothered with reciprocal arrangements. Too much trouble! So it's a one way street.

Enough of the politics. What does this tell me? Simple! The USA is the best tax haven in the world for foreigners! The USA is not the least bit harassed by the OECD with all of the 'black list' and 'grey list' B.S. which they impose on everyone else.

This is great for foreigners! The U.S. treats foreigners better than its own citizens. What about Americans? Americans can benefit using simple logic. Set up a parallel existence as we just discussed. Those foreign 'persons' can come back into the USA with all the special advantages that Americans don't have at home, nor have abroad.

Through your legitimate business relationship with 'those persons' they can help you do great things in business and finance right in your own back yard. Amazing 'eh?

So, what we have here is a wonderful opportunity for Americans to use their own back yard as the 'Best Tax Haven' in the world!!

How do you like them apples? Ha!

In fact, I know a U.S. attorney who specializes in working with 'foreigners' who want to do business in the USA and he has some pretty interesting capabilities.

Many of his clients are not foreigners at all, but are Americans, just like you! Imagine that.

Just some food for thought to put in the pot and stir a bit!

"Cast out the slave and her son; for the son of the slave shall not inherit with the son of the free woman."
- Galatians 4:30

CHAPTER 9

THE C.F.R.

VERY FEW 'LAYPEOPLE' HAVE EVER heard of the C.F.Rs., which is the 'Code of Federal Regulations'. Don't fall asleep! This gets really good! The C.F.Rs. are the implementing regulations which give the statutes their enforceability. In other words the C.F.R.s are the teeth in the legislative code.

The courts have ruled consistently, as in the Supreme Court decision in California Bankers Association v. Shultz 416 US 21 (1974), that a statute without a corresponding C.F.R. is unenforceable.

In legal research, when the legislature passes a new law, it is recorded in the 'Sessions Laws'. This is where you can find the organic law and the original intent of the legislatures. Interestingly enough this can differ from what is eventually 'codified' in the statutes and I've had some fun with that.

Those Sessions Laws, otherwise referred to as the 'Statutes at Large' are re-written and codified and then become part of the 'statutory law' which is found in the U.S. Code (U.S.C.).

In the U.S., federal law is passed by the Congress. Those statutes then must have corresponding C.F.R.s written to be implemented and to be enforceable.

With this basic understanding, and it's all we need here, whenever I've been addressed by the IRS in their correspondence and they refer to my legal obligations in relation to Title 26 of the U.S.C., which is the

Internal Revenue Code or I.R.C. I immediately look up the referenced statute in the <u>Parallel Table of Authorities and Rules</u> which gives quick reference to each statute and it's corresponding C.F.R.

You'd be amazed what can be found in here. The C.F.R.s are a virtual playground for truth seekers and trouble makers like me. Why? They expose the pure fallacy of what the IRS is trying to get you to believe.

The C.F.R.s reveal in black and white that the big, omnipotent, loud, scary, all seeing, all knowing, fire breathing wizard of dominance and control is nothing more than a silly little, stunted man behind a curtain pulling the levers of fraud and deception to get us to cower in fear and submit to his every whim! You want proof? Look at this.

There are hundreds of examples but let me give you a just a couple right now for illustration purposes:

26 USC 7201	Attempt to evade or defeat tax	No regulation
26 USC 6212	Notice of deficiency	No regulation
26 USC 6201	Assessment authority	27 CFR part 70
26 USC 6303	Notice and demand for tax	27 CFR part 70
26 USC 6321	Lien for taxes	27 CFR part 70
26 USC 6331	Levy & Distraint	27 CFR part 70
26 USC 6332	Surrender of property subject to levy	27 CFR part 70
26 USC 7203	Wilful failure to file return	No regulation

26 USC 7343	Definition of term 'person'	No regulation
26 USC 7603	Service of summons	27 CFR part 70

I could write an entire book on only what this chart represents, and nothing more. What does '27 CFR part 70' mean? Let's back up. Title 26 is the Internal Revenue Code. All matters of the so called 'income tax' which the IRS wants to put on your shoulders are contained in Title 26. A proper implementing regulation would also relate to title 26 in the C.F.R.

So what is Title 27? Title 27 relates 'exclusively' to 'Alcohol, Tobacco and Firearms'. All Title 27 statutes and regulations are exclusive to the 'excise taxes' imposed on the various classes of manufacturers, distributors and retailers engaged in the business of alcohol, tobacco and firearms.

So what does that have to do with Title 26? Nothing! Get it? What this table of authorities is telling me is that the only enforcement authority which the law allows, when the C.F.R. relates to title 27, is the enforcement of ATF activity ONLY and nothing else.

So when the IRS threatens me with 26 USC 6321, a 'Lien for taxes' I would first confirm that the implementing authority only relates to Title 27 and then immediately challenge that presumption and demand documentary evidence of my involvement in alcohol, tobacco or firearms. Failure on their part destroys their original presumption and offensive attack. I would give them 30 days to respond and when they don't, set the record as we have done previously.

They are using the same tricks on you! When they accuse you (by sleight of hand) of activity relating to Title 27, and through your ignorance you fail to object, then you have agreed with the presumption and 'their record' is set!

See how that works? Through your silence and failure to object, you have 'agreed' and they then proceed against you accordingly with your consent! Don't ever let their correspondence go unanswered because you'll be accepting all kinds of assumptions and presumptions which probably don't apply to you!

Are you starting to see how they operate? So if you are involved in a business involving alcohol, tobacco or firearms, then this may apply to you! If not, well, you can draw your own conclusions.

What does it mean when it says 'no regulation'?

Simple. The courts have ruled that the statute is unenforceable and has no effect. It is equivalent to 'non-existence'.

Yet people all over the land take from their families, to give their 'fair share' to the grand, almighty wizard, to pay 'obligations' which don't even exist by law, but are created with your approval consent.

All I can say is...Wow!

"My people perish for lack of knowledge:
because thou hast rejected knowledge,
I will also reject thee."
Hosea 4:6

CHAPTER 10

ACCEPTED FOR VALUE

'ACCEPTANCE FOR VALUE' (A4V OR AFV) has become a veritable movement of its own as you will see if you do a simple search on YouTube. The power it wields relates to the fact that it is simply an advanced under-standing and application of the commercial code which we now know is the law of the land for everybody.

The benefit of this body of knowledge on commercial law is that you have the ability to tap into a 'pre-paid' account, and that with your signature and a proper 'presentment' you can discharge not only your tax bills, bank debt, credit cards, mortgages and other 'credit' but you can also use this same legal technology to 'discharge' a criminal complaint.

This is not some new toy, trick or process that somebody just came up with. It has been 'the law' since the law has been on the books. It hasn't been until recently, that researchers have uncovered the secrets and put them into practice with positive results for 'individuals'.

It's going to be difficult for me to explain this in a way that makes sense in this short format without a proper in depth study of it's history and the issues involved. We can't do that here. It gets a bit deep.

So let me hit just some of the high points involved to give you an outline, with the understanding that this explanation will likely leave you with more questions than answers, and we'll just have to leave it at that for now. There are plenty of resources available for a continuation of your study should you choose to follow those.

If this is all new to you, let me warn you, it will seem a bit far fetched and foreign to your way of thinking. But by now, if you've properly absorbed the contents of this book to this point, you likely realize that your way of thinking up until now has probably been a bit behind the curve with 'reality' in terms of how the law operates. Am I correct?

We can start with a definition provided by USlegal.com:

"Acceptance for value is a commercial right that is obtained through instruments such as tax bills and violation tickets. It is a qualified endorsement or modified signature on an instrument. By accepting an instrument for value, one becomes the holder in due course of the instrument and can enforce the instrument on the issuer.

As per U.C.C. § 3-303, an instrument is issued or transferred for value if:

1) the instrument is issued or transferred for a promise of performance, to the extent the promise has been performed;
2) the transferee acquires a security interest or other lien in the instrument other than a lien obtained by judicial proceeding;
3) the instrument is issued or transferred as payment of, or as security for, an antecedent claim against any person, whether or not the claim is due;
4) the instrument is issued or transferred in exchange for a negotiable instrument; or
5) the instrument is issued or transferred in exchange for the incurring of an irrevocable obligation to a third party by the person taking the instrument.

'Acceptance' and 'Acceptance for Value' is not the same. Accepting an instrument without a qualified endorsement waives all defects there may be in the instrument, including the value, or lack of value, that comes with it. Accepting an instrument for value and returning it is notice to the issuer that the endorser is not providing new value, but is converting the issuer's obligation to pay the instrument into the value, thereby making the instrument negotiable." -End of definition

Now then, let's unravel this and see how powerful it is. In commerce, when a presentment is made (i.e. a bill, demand for payment, etc) The U.C.C. (Uniform Commercial Code) governs the handling of those 'negotiable instruments'.

Since 1933 when HJR 192 was passed by Congress and removed the gold backing of our money, the country has been in a perpetual state of bankruptcy. There is no lawful money in circulation and debts cannot be 'paid' at law, in substance.

What we have now is a system of using negotiable instruments and bills of exchange in commerce. The 'Federal Reserve Note', is a promissory note (promise to pay in the future) but is not redeemable and is never paid. Does that make sense so far?

I like to have fun with this one. I like to go into a restaurant and run up a nice tab. When the waitress brings the bill, I tell her with a look of sadness on my face that I really enjoyed the meal and the service, but that I don't have any money and all I can give her for payment is a 'promise to pay' which will never be paid.

After getting over her confusion she'll have to go get the manager. When the manager comes out, this is always a great opportunity to break out my 'Federal Reserve Notes' and educate the two on how worthless the money is and that this is all you have to settle the bill with. Again, they look confused, but they eventually get the point and with a friendly discussion, you could actually educate someone and have a couple of laughs!

The medium of exchange (money) which we use is 'credit' via negotiable instruments: notes, bonds, certificates, obligations of insurance, annuities, bills of exchange, etc.

The entire system is built on <u>promises</u> which is 'debt'.

Now let's go back to the time of your birth. Since this system has been in place, when baby John Doe is born, his mother's 'water' breaks (upon the water (seas) he is in Admiralty law) he is 'born' onto the land in Admiralty, then 'delivered' (as chattel property) into the world of commerce and into the hands of the state, via the Birth 'Certificate'. I know, it sounds a little weird but it is very significant and there is more to it than meets the eye.

No longer do we use a simple 'Certificate of Live Birth' which applies to John Doe the individual. But the new 'Birth Certificate', with the 'seal of authentication' using baby Doe's feet is submitted and created as baby <u>JOHN DOE</u> trust account and the new 'legal person' (corporate fiction) is 'registered' as a security and delivered into the world of commerce.

The Birth Certificate has a serial number and this then becomes a registered security or 'negotiable instrument' in the form of a bond which is deposited for the benefit of the U.S. Treasury. The monetary value of this 'bond' is quite significant. Stop and consider all the future fees, fines and taxes that JOHN DOE will pay over his lifetime. He is worth quite a hefty sum!

There is a great video on this subject on the 'Resources' page of www.onefreemanswar.com You need to see it for a clear understanding.

Now, add to that the concept that 'credit' (money) is created not by the government, not by the Federal Reserve, but by 'the people'. The people are 'sponsors of the credit'. In addition to creating a highly valuable bond at birth, every time you sign a credit card agreement, mortgage note, or other promise to pay, 'You' have created money! Remember, money is 'debt'! When you make a promise to pay, you have created debt and debt is money!

An entire chapter of my book ONE FREEMAN'S WAR IN THE SECOND AMERICAN REVOLUTION is devoted to how one high level C.P.A. has determined, using modern accounting methods, that all bank loans are fraud because the bank doesn't lend their own money as advertised. They charge you fees, take your collateral and after you create the money with the promissory note, and give it to them, they deposit it as an asset on the books and lend it back to you as check book money. This is illegal conversion and accounting fraud. That's another story which we get into in the other book.

The point is that 'you' create money when you add to the 'credit' and 'negotiable instruments' in circulation. You are the 'sponsor of the credit' which gives you great power!

Therefore, as it relates to the Accepted for Value process, as 'sponsor of the credit' you, John Doe, can take charge of the pre-paid account (bond/registered security) which is JOHN DOE and with your signature, you honor all presentments, accept them for value as per the U.C.C. and have that presentment (debt, bill, demand) discharged by virtue of your authorization (qualified signature) to tap that pre-paid account linked to your bond.

Again, I've taken a full treatise of law and tried to condense it down to a couple pages, which just doesn't work well. But hopefully you have picked up on some of the key points here to see how the law can be used by those who choose to learn it for their benefit.

How does this relate to the I.R.S.?

Whenever they send a 'Notice of Tax Deficiency' and 'Demand for Payment of Tax' in any form, it may be 'accepted for value' (honored) and returned as a negotiable instrument with permission and instructions to have it paid from your pre-paid account!

Done!

I know it sounds crazy if this is all new to you, but guess what? Many people have done it with success! Why does it work? Because it's the law! Are you ready to learn?

CHAPTER 11

FUN AND FRAUD
WITH DEFINITIONS

JUST FOR FUN, LET'S TAKE a look at the definitions in the Internal Revenue Code. Again, these are the federal statutes in Title 26 of the U.S. Code. For starters, let's look at 26 USC 7701 (a)(9), (10), (26) & (31).

Sec. 7701. Definitions

(A) When used in this title, where not otherwise distinctly expressed or manifestly incompatible with the intent thereof.

    (9)   **United States.** The term "United States" when used in a geographic sense includes only the states and the District of Columbia.

   (10) **State**. The term "state" shall be construed to include the District of Columbia.

   (26) **Trade or Business**. The term "Trade or Business" includes the performance of the functions of public office.

   (31) **Foreign Estate or Trust**. the terms "foreign estate or trust" mean an estate or trust...the income of which from sources without the United States which is not effectively connected

with the conduct of a 'trade or business' within the United States, is not includable in gross income under subtitle A.

Interesting. Let's understand some basics here. In law when you see the term 'includes' you can take it to mean 'only', or 'at the exclusion of anything else not mentioned'.

So then with definition (10) in mind which says that the term 'state' shall be construed to 'include' (only) the District of Columbia, we can now look at (9) and interpret that to say: "The term Unites States.... includes only the District of Columbia." And (26) is clear that Trade or Business is 'only' performing the functions of public office. Are you catching on?

So then, based only on 'definitions' in the law, we can clearly see that unless you are engaged in the performance of a public office in Washington, D.C., you would likely be considered a 'Foreign Estate or Trust' whose income is not includable in gross income under subtitle A of the I.R.C.

Did you ever think that studying the law could be so much fun?

CHAPTER 12

DO WHAT THE BANKERS DO!

YOU KNOW WE'RE INVOLVED IN the game of 'commerce' and 'banking' and perhaps it all seems a bit daunting at times. That would only be because you don't understand the rules of the game like the 'professionals' do. Well, the only solution to that is for you to become as proficient as the professionals and use the simple rules of the game to your advantage. It's not that difficult. Let me give you an example.

When the bank takes your money (promissory note/credit) and loans it back to you with interest, pretending that it's a 'loan', what do they do? To secure their interest in the loan (your money in the first place by way of the note you gave them) they place a lien on the property to secure their (fraudulent) interest. If that property is ever sold, they get their money first and nobody can jump ahead of them in line! It's simple banking and commerce and everybody understands how that works.

So why don't you use the same procedure to protect yourself?

Let's say that maybe you've had enough harassment by the IRS, or you just don't intend to offer them any satisfaction just in case, someday down the road, they want to get ugly with you. You want to plan for a rainy day and sleep peacefully at night.

You can set up a legitimate business arrangement with a friendly company to secure everything you have. The way it works is simple. A services contract can be negotiated in which that company has a legitimate claim and to secure that claim, they put a lien on the equity in your property. Whoever comes along after the fact, will have to step in line to take what's left *after* the lien is first satisfied with the friendly company.

Let me tell you a real story that happened to a friend of mine where he used this successfully. My friend Paul was running a thriving small package delivery service. He did everything by the book. Had all his licenses, insurance, permits, workman's compensation set up, the whole ball of wax. His business was doing well and he thrived for the first couple of years and built a new home for himself and his family from his profits.

Then one day a state bureau-rat came along and made a visit. The bureau-rat wanted to inspect his papers, permits, insurance, etc. Everything seemed in order. That was, until the bureau-rat started talking about wanting to reclassify the business' status in the workman's comp program.

Currently, the business was paying the premium which was appropriate for 'small packages' up to 25 pounds. That's all they handled. That was their business.

The bureau-rat started talking about re-classifying the business as one which handled packages up to 100 pounds on the basis that, even though it wasn't a current need, it's possible that it *could be* in the future. This 'adjustment' would have skyrocketed Paul's premiums.

So a bureaucratic fight ensued over the next few months and Paul was staunchly defending his position that he was properly classified and had no need or interest in handling larger packages.

During this fight, he started to sense that he wasn't going to prevail. And not only that, but the government was talking about making this re-classification retroactive **nunc pro tunc,** back to the beginning of his business, a couple of years prior.

This would have created a huge financial liability which Paul had no ability or intention to ever pay. Do you see how the mafia works whenever they want to do a little 'fundraising'?

He was particularly concerned that the new dream home that he had just built for his family would be in jeopardy if he were forced to pay, and that was his primary concern.

So what did Paul do? We studied the issue together and he quickly decided to become a banker and do what bankers do.

He found a company who was interested in using him for his fiduciary services. This fiduciary responsibility had a monetary value which required security of some sort. So he had to come up with a 'deposit' or 'guarantee'. We could even call it a 'performance bond', to secure the company's interest in the contract which the two had created. If he were to default in his duties, or cause damage to the company in the exercise thereof, the company could look to the guarantee to satisfy the contract.

Since he didn't have cash or other assets, he used the equity in his new dream home and he gave the company a lien position on his property. The contract was executed and the lien was filed properly in the county recorders office to secure the company's interest.

Subsequent to that, the state made a final determination on his workman's comp re-classification. It was settled that he was being re-classified, the premiums were being adjusted nunc pro tunc, and he had a huge bill staring him in the face for over $100,000. He didn't know whether to laugh or cry out loud.

He decided to tell the government to go F**K off, he closed the business, liquidated everything and decided to sell his home and leave the state entirely. He had no intention of living in a land where it was open season on business owners as he had just experienced.

The beautiful house sold quickly. The lien holder showed up at the closing and collected a check for their part of the equity. From that point on, let's just say that Paul and his counterpart to the contract which held the lien and received the check were able to make some additional business transactions which were quite suitable to Paul and his young family.

The entire experience left a sour taste in Paul's mouth as you can well imagine. But he surely had the benefit and relief of knowing that he mitigated the damage of the state by staying 'one step ahead'. The state had ruined his business, but it didn't touch his family or their security. His foresight enabled him to start over somewhere else with the business profits invested wisely in his home, which he recovered 100% of!

The bankers have all the advantages, right? Maybe you could become a banker too!

CHAPTER 13

DECODING THE IMF

WHAT IF... JUST 'WHAT IF' the IRS were collecting taxes from you on the false assumption and presumption that you owed the 'excise' tax which was due according to law, as it relates to 'Rum Distillers' located in the U.S. Virgin Islands (federal territory) as outlined in Title 27 of the USC and the CFRs (not Title 26 as the IRS 'pretends')?

Would it be appropriate to 'object' to the false presumption and thereby destroy any attempts by the I.R.S. to collect such tax from you, and put it upon the IRS to provide evidence of any 'other' taxable activity which they may have in their records in which you are engaged?

The simple fact of the matter is that I and many thousands of people have done FOIA (Freedom of Information Act) requests to receive their 'Individual Master File' (IMF) and have had them 'decoded' only to find that we were classified with a false and fraudulent 'er *erroneous* 'tax code' TC 150 (Rum Distiller in federal territory) or something similarly and completely inaccurate and inappropriate.

Remember that in law, failure to object is fatal. And if you don't object to being classified as a Rum Distiller from Puerto Rico, or the US Virgin Islands, then you have agreed and you must be! And you 'should' pay that tax!

"The IRS maintains electronic records about you in their computer system called the Integrated Document Retrieval System (IDRS) and the Audit Information Management System (AIMS)

- There are five main types of records IRS maintains in their IDRS system:
  - BusinessMasterFiles (BMF): Tracks businesses
  - Individual Master File (IMF): Tracks individuals
  - Non Master File (NMF): Tracks things that don't fit in other files, along with manual assessments – Employee Plans Master File (EPMF): Tracks employee retirement plans
  - Individual Retirement Account File (IRAF): Tracks Individual Retirement Accounts – Information Return Master File (IRMF): Tracks 1099's, W-2's, etc.

  All IRS records are maintained in large computer mainframes distributed throughout the country

  - All data is batch processed weekly at each computer center
  - The computer centers stay synchronized by sending information files from around the country into the Martinsburg Computing Center (MCC).

Information is recorded using cryptic alphanumeric codes that are not understandable without access to the "code books" and IRS training and reference materials

- All IRS records about you are available by simply requesting them under the Privacy Act, 5 U.S.C. §552a and the Freedom of Information Act (FOIA), 5 U.S.C. §552
- IRS is very secretive and protective of information that could be used to help educate people about the meaning of information in these files because:
  - Knowing what the IRS knows about you eliminates your fear of them, which removes an important means of leverage they use to intimidate us
  - Mishandling or illegal falsification of files by IRS employees can result in personal liability for criminal and civil lawsuits

- These files allow you to invalidate illegal assessments by the IRS, which means they become uncollectible and must be fixed.

The specific purposes of IMF decoding are precisely as follows:

- Understand everything the IRS "thinks" they know about you
- Discover whether their information about you is false or fraudulent
- Administratively correct any false, fraudulent, or inaccurate information
- Identify violations of statutes, regulations, and internal procedures
- Provide evidence proving that assessments against you are illegal and therefore invalid
- Expose, prevent, or circumvent illegal collection activity
- Provide you with information that is useful in responding to illegal or improper IRS letters and notices
- Identify specific IRS employees who are falsifying your records and violating tax statutes, regulations, and internal procedures so they can be prosecuted with a Bivens Action
- Produce evidence of IRS wrongdoing that you can send in to the IRS to have entered into your official IRS administrative record which will immunize you from subsequent illegal criminal or civil prosecution."

The above information/quote is provided by our friends at sedm.org

We have clear proof that the I.R.S. is deliberately trying to hide this information from the public. They don't want you to know what is in your IMF!

We have to ask ourselves, that if the IRS were a lawful organization merely executing the bona fide laws of the land, what would they have to hide? Why shouldn't all legal matters be 100% transparent to the people whom the public servants serve?

Is it possible that the I.R.S. is NOT executing a lawful collection of taxes?

Could it be possible that they are hiding deliberate and willful attempts of fraudulent conversion of private assets based on fraudulent presumptions?

Could it be that the public officials directing and condoning this activity (all elected public officials who have sworn an oath) and who stand by giving consent by their silence, are violating their oaths of office and committing treason and sedition?

Is it possible that what they are collecting are not 'taxes' at all (according to law) but instead they are coercing the people through fear, intimidation and ignorance to make voluntary 'donations' as a part of a socialist experiment at 'social redistribution' to serve political ends which are fully entrenched in socialist, or communist philosophies?

If any of this were true, would it be 'American'? or 'Satanic'?

It's up to you to come up with your own answers, but only after you fully research and understand the issues raised in this book.

Perhaps then, you'll be able to join me when I say... "I Beat Satan... and the I.R.S.!"

CHAPTER 14

WHAT NEXT?

WELL, I'VE TRIED TO KEEP this short and sweet. If I've done anything, I hope that I've blown the lid off of your previously held notions of 'reality'.

The net effect of that could be, that if enough of us can become educated on these matters, the little man behind the curtain could soon be out of business and we might have a chance to restore some hope for the futures of our families, our communities and of our nation.

But that will take some work. It will take all of us shutting off the T.V., picking up the books, educating ourselves, sharing information and helping others to follow in your path as you follow in my path and as I have followed the paths laid down by others. If you feel the same way, you need to share this book. Momentum is building!

And when you know who you are, as a child of God, and embrace the essence of what that means, you'll find that fear dissipates. Strength, determination and courage grows and you know that no matter what happens, you win in the end! Now isn't that a much better way to live than in the alternative?

I am only a messenger. I have learned these things from others and perhaps I am silly or stupid enough to actually put them into practice for myself just to 'see what would happen'. Yet, so far (25 years and counting) I have prevailed in the big picture and have been blessed so many times over I cannot count them all.

If you care to continue on this path with me, then I would highly recommend that you expand your foundational understanding of some of the key issues with the book previously referenced.   It can be found on www.onefreemanswar.com

After that, I and some associates are creating a new educational resource called the LIGHTHOUSE LAW CLUB which will be a resource center for people interested in the truth, the law and the prospects for achieving liberty, security and prosperity for all!   You can find that at www.lighthouseliberty.club

"For the kingdom of God does not consist of talk, but of power. "
-1 Corinthians 4:20

ABOUT THE AUTHOR

MARK EMERY HAS HAD A life rich in experience on many fronts. His zeal for making bold moves and pushing the envelope of the status quo has, at times, gotten him into trouble. He is not afraid to ruffle feathers. But his real life adventures always leave an imprint with somebody, somewhere. As an international entrepreneur he is self made, he has travelled the world, and he has an in depth knowledge of international relations, finance, law, travel, language and culture. Back home in the states, he comes from a successful business background where his avocation in law led him to be a public speaker, radio talk show host and a popular activist fighting for truth and justice. Thankfully, he feels compelled to share his experiences and knowledge through his writing. His aim is that this will make a positive difference in someone's life, and perhaps spark some new flames of passion for law and truth after he is long gone.

Made in the USA
Coppell, TX
04 May 2020

24065384R00044